# This Is Me Now

I0159293

Lindsay Brant-Brumwell

This Is Me Now

Copyright © 2013 Lindsay Brant-Brumwell  (Brand New Content)

# Table of Contents

Dedication

Willows Weep     1

The Bottle     2

Barricade Warrior     4

Listen to my Story     6

Trapped     7

Words     8

Blood Not Divided     9

I could be that Indian     10

For Birds Unknown     11

A Free Bird Flies     12

We Sang It Too     13

This is Me Now     15

Buried Blood     17

Navigating Me     19

Ask Her     21

We Give Thanks                                          23

Promise Made                                            25

Internal River                                         28

Arrived                                                29

# Dedication

Firstly, I dedicate this poetry collection to my family who has always believed in me and supported my need for expression of self through the written word. This is for my parents, for teaching me to be true to myself, and to treat others with kindness always. To my Mom, thank you for teaching me that belief in myself must come before all other gifts in life. To my Dad, who once said that I saved his life, you co-created mine, so let's call it even!

To my husband, and sons. Thank you for always holding a mirror up to me, and asking me to look deeply into it, so that I may reflect that woman back to you. Thank you to my husband for always loving me for who I am, and in moments when I felt I couldn't love myself, he was kind enough to love me enough for both of us. Thank you also for teaching me that your love cannot replace self-love and that I must develop and nourish this as well.

Secondly, I dedicate this poetry collection to the members of my beloved community, Tyendinaga Mohawk Territory, and the Aboriginal community at large. I hope that you find pieces of yourselves reflected within these poems and that they may offer you support and healing as you read them, such as they have provided me during the writing process. Nia:wen kowa (A big thank you).

# Willows Weep

Bark-stained tears fall

And gather under trunk

The forest.

A chorus of pain

Willows weep

Hearts of my people

reflected there

In bark-stained tears

A distorted image:

Broken lakes

Blood red

Amongst the green

# The Bottle

Raised to lips

Not of whispered I love yous

Peering through glass

A face not recognizable

Bottle raised to lips

Not speaking of what will drown

Pain, sorrow, loss,

Go down smooth tonight

In the morning light

Will things appear differently?

Smell of stale beer

seeping through pores

Stop

Wait

Bottle breaks

Shattered

Pieces there

Looking for a new way

Bottle raised to lips

No more

# Barricade Warrior

Barricade warrior,

Look at who you are fencing in!

United in separation

From yourself, your people

What is the real issue here?

Could it be just beyond the fear?

Walls cannot talk

Until they fall away

Then and only then

Can we find a new way

Barricade warrior,

Look at what you are fencing in!

For countless days of freeze and thaw

of anger, hurt, tears

Walls cannot talk

Until they fall away

Then and only then

Can we find a way

Barricade warrior,

Lead your people to a new day

# Listen to my Story

Please listen to my story,

It's the only one I know.

It starts inside. It builds. Builds, and builds.

It requires you to grow.

My story needs a listener,

To make it come alive.

Please listen to my story,

and help it to survive.

But once you've heard my story,

don't pretend it was never told.

Take my story, for now it is yours to hold

Now that you have my story,

spread it around Mother Earth

Your telling it will heal me,

And you will contribute to its birth.

# Trapped

There is no answer.

They don't want to

Come out today.


Moments like these are not so free,

they're filled with tiny cells

full of words

I wish to break out


Don't you want to break out?

Together we can be free

# Words

Words not superseding,

Race relations depleting,

Silence has so much meaning.

I think we need to talk.

There is so much misunderstanding.

Mistruths that need grounding.

Hearts that need surrounding.

I think we need to talk.


Words now filled with meaning.

Race relations are succeeding.

Broken hearts begin healing.

We've found a way to talk.

# Blood Not Divided

My blood is not divided.

I am not *half* anything.

I am a whole being.

All that is in my blood,

Makes me –

Who I am.

Half is not less.

Two halves make a whole,

And my life is richer for the mix.

# I could be that Indian

I could be that Indian,

That lives in the tipi.

I could be that Indian,

That you see on T.V.

I could be that Indian,

Stoic and grave.

I could be that Indian,

Mascot of the Atlanta Braves.

I could be that Indian,

That you already think I am.

I could be that Indian,

The one you want me to be.

But I'd rather not,

I'd prefer to be just me.

# For Birds Unknown

From birds unknown a song rings out

Sad and out of tune

Nobody there to listen

There is nothing they can do

But sing and sing their sad song

And hope that it rings through

That someone will hear it

And help them change the tune.

# A Free Bird Flies

A free bird flies

As far as the longing in her wings

A free bird flies

Carrying with her a tune to sing

A free bird flies

Beyond the horizon of her sight

A free bird flies

Freeing others with her flight

# We Sang It Too

One little, two little...

The words echo in my head.

You know the song.

Well, we sang it too.

Enska, Tekeni, Ahsen, niha':ti,

Kaie:ri, Wisk tanon Ia':iak Oni.

Tsia:ta, Sha'te:kon, Tiohton, Oie:ri,

Niha':ti onkwehon'we

Maybe it was the only song we knew

With Indians in it.

We sang it just to hear our own name.

But that is not the name we want –

It's the name we've been given.

So why did we sing it?

Did we think we could somehow

13

Change that little Indian?

Make him our own?

I don't know if that Indian has changed

It must be time for a new song.

# This is Me Now

Hey, this is Me Now.

I am telling you for the first time,

This is Me Now.

I know for the first time,

This is Me Now.

I can feel for the first time,

This is Me Now.

I see for the first time,

This is Me Now.

Where I am meant to be now.

I can be free now.

Hey, this is Me Now.

I'm thanking you for allowing me to be now,

Who I've always been before,

But never really saw how,

I could say,

Hey, this is Me Now.

# Buried Blood

Half breed, half breed, half breed

They'd tease

He buried the blood that day

So deep his children wouldn't find it

They need not feel the blood

Coursing through their veins

It would only bring pain

Something, a longing you might say,

Led them to find the blood that way

He was gone,

But the blood remained

For them to try on,

To see how it feels,

And...

They buried the blood that day,

Deep within their veins

A new part of them

Was found

Buried underground

And now they wear it

Proud

# Navigating Me

Why must I always navigate

Through and in between

Force the two extremes

Mohawk or White

You say

Forcing me to choose

When I pick a side

An identity must hide

And we all stand to lose

Why can't I celebrate

My hyphen -

my slash /

my and

my or

Don't place me in a box

That I don't see a reason for!

# Ask Her

Ask her

Why she's angry

And she'll say

It's because you

took her voice away

A once live and vibrant spirit

Crushed

A proud existence

Hushed


Ask her

Why she's angry

And she'll say

It's because you

Took her voice away

At a school known

As an Indian Day


You tried to

Break her

Take her

Make her

Lose her way

At a school known as the Indian Day

# We Give Thanks

We give thanks

For all of creation

So that we may

Express our heart's content

For all things

Seen and unseen

Blessings the creator has sent

Gratitude keeps us humble

It keeps us in a space

Where we are open

To being present

And accepting of our place

The reason for our existence

Our place on Mother Earth

Becomes so very apparent

But it begins with

Nia:wen

first.

# Promise Made

I am determined to keep a promise made,

So my sons will learn to trust.

If their faith in me is what I seek,

Then honesty is a must.

I hate an empty promise,

Words spoken but not kept.

In my childhood,

Broken promises

are sometimes why I wept.


Daddy didn't mean to promise me,

The things he couldn't give,

but the bottle was much stronger,

that drink could reel him in

he would forget about a promise made,

forget just what he said

to a little girl who's Daddy

was the centre of her heart

a promise made,

meant everything,

and a broken one tore her apart!


My whole world was shattered

Each time he'd tell me not today,

He would never ever hurt me intentionally,

This never was his way!

But the bottle was much stronger,

That drink could reel him in

In a sudden lapse in judgement,

He'd forget about a promise made,

and the little girl who looked up to him.


I forgive you Daddy,

I blame the bottle now

My unconditional love for you remains

At the centre of my heart

I hope the bottle
smashes.

I hope it falls apart.

I will be there to help you,

This is my promise made.

Let's let the healing start.

# Internal River

She sat by a river to clear her head,

But her thoughts started speaking to her instead.

One of her thoughts told her,

That river is just like me,

Only I am the kind that flows internally.

I can lead you to where you have always longed to be.

I can help you find your destiny.

My rapids will not throw you off course,

unless you lose sight of what matters most.

Along your journey,

Through the currents, and whistling wind,

Please listen to me,

Your newly discovered friend,

The river that flows within.

# Arrived

I long for that moment,

Where I can say that I've arrived,

I'm exactly where I wanted to be,

I've held back nothing,

I've swallowed my pride.

I wonder if I will know it,

When that moment comes my way

What will I think, what will I feel?

Will I weep or will I pray?

Will I be happy in that moment?

Or will I look to jump again,

To reach a new horizon,

To say I can be more,

This is the moment I am always striving for.


This is the moment that I want for all of us,

A celebration of culture,

Identity restored

To say we have survived;

Our people have arrived!